THE POWER OF CONNECTION

THE POWER OF CONNECTION

Building Meaningful Relationships

HARPER NORTHWOOD

QuillQuest Publishers

CONTENTS

1 Introduction 1

2 Understanding Connection 4

3 Building Strong Foundations 6

4 Communication Skills 8

5 Emotional Intelligence 10

6 Cultivating Trust 13

7 Resolving Conflict 15

8 Nurturing Relationships Over Time 18

9 The Role of Technology 20

10 Building Professional Relationships 23

11 Relationships in Different Contexts 26

12 Cultural Considerations 28

13 The Impact of Social Media 30

14 Mentorship and Guidance 32

15 Self-Reflection and Growth 35

16 The Power of Gratitude 37

17   Conclusion   40

CHAPTER 1

Introduction

In this twenty-first century, we are living in a world full of gadgets and super-fast communication technology. We can get news of our loved ones within seconds from every corner of the world. We can manage our business, pay our utility bills, and purchase anything - all within a matter of seconds while sitting at our home. Everybody is busy. Everybody is busy with his or her BlackBerrys, iPods, iPads, iPhones, etc. At the same time, an interesting development has caught our attention. Despite being in touch with a vast number of people (both relatives and friends), personal interaction among people at large has suffered significantly. We fear that our children have lost their capabilities of building real and meaningful relationships with each other and with their families. A decade has passed since we started using mobile phones; it has been over half a decade since we began using iPhones, the gadget that made it possible to provide dual services (phone and Internet). The purpose for using these smart gadgets was to make life easier so that we have more time to spend on important tasks, like making the relationship between people meaningful.

The Importance of Meaningful Relationships

When people are asked about their social connections, we often use the word "relationship" to describe different things. For example, many people are very active on social media, connecting with hundreds or even thousands of other people, some of whom they might not even have met. This is just one way in which people can be connected. We might also experience brief yet positive interactions with strangers. In the workplace, for example, we see thousands of people every year, and sometimes we might share warm moments with them. In contrast, people are likely to have just a handful of very close friends. These are the people we would describe as "knowing us well" and being "important to our personal lives". We can think of the term "meaningful relationship" encompassing the people who are closest to us—our friends and family—while excluding the larger circle of acquaintances. But are these meaningful relationships important?

Clinical research tells us that our social connections play an important role in our health and well-being. In an influential meta-analysis, Julianne Holt-Lunstad and her colleagues looked at data from 148 studies including over 300,000 people across an average of 7.5 years. They found that the risk of death for people with stronger social relationships was 50 percent higher than the risk of death for those with weaker social connections. Put another way, people with strong social relationships lived an average of 3.7 years longer than those with weaker relationships. This makes social relationships as large a contributing factor to our health as smoking, alcohol abuse, and physical inactivity. Researchers have proposed various reasons why social relationships make such a difference. For example, strong social relationships have been linked to improved immune function, reduced inflammation, and metabolic regulation. They also provide important social support during difficult times, helping to buffer the negative effects of stress. But do all social connections help us in the same way?

CHAPTER 2

Understanding Connection

A spiritual connection to God provides a deeper, more profound relationship than any other relationship on earth. Remember, though, this is about finding our way to make us happy. Meaningful relationships are essential to our happiness and, indeed, to human existence. We feel our soul when we connect with a spirituality that is more significant and more powerful than us. That is not to imply that religious ties are a must for a cheerful heart. Whatever that looks like in our life, it's good for us to affiliate and connect. Being close to God gives us confidence and happiness. It's only after we spend time nurturing our energies with the Creator inside of us by heightening our spirituality that we can achieve our greatest potential and live a life full of joy.

So, what's the bottom line? What does the power of human connection do for us when we are on the receiving end? Humans desperately crave social interaction and need it to feel close and wanted. When we are in touch with others physically, emotionally, or spiritually, our lives are more joyful. When we hold hands or our spouse gives us a kind touch, we feel a connection between us and that other person. When we are with our spiritual, strong people, we are in our happy place. Many times, we hide our God self from others because it is personal and protected, but we miss out on some beautiful human interaction as a result. We miss a chance to feel fully happy and content.

Defining Connection

Brené Brown has found that the main characteristic in forming a connection with others is having one thing in common: the feeling of a deep sense of safety and a sense of worthiness, which will promote a sense of security within the relationship. Indeed, the presence of emotional security is conducive to the process of connection and romantic love and helps the pair bond and coordinate with one another. The couple can rely on each other and mutually exchange their thoughts and emotions, giving them a sense of identity and security. Concurrently, the research shows that there is a positive correlation between security, verbal cues, and emotional strong connections. As aforementioned, connections are influenced by various factors which can be classified into three patterns, which are inward, other-directed, and outward.

Connection is defined as a relationship in which a person or a thing is linked or associated with something else. It is the attitude of caring about others and the quality of the relationships in which people are experiencing the involvement and mutual influence with others, thus assisting them in reaching a common goal, as well as helping them to realize their true potential or to be what they want to be. According to Brown, connections occur within the relationship when individuals are genuinely interested and are involved in the life of the counterpart. It is about authenticity and being true to oneself, as well as being able to talk honestly, have a sense of oneself and self-worth.

CHAPTER 3

Building Strong Foundations

The elements required to build strong foundations in a relationship are the groundwork of strengths which will ensure positive growth, long-lasting durability and the lifting of individual capacity and organizational potential. Together they create the atmosphere within which comfort, confidence and a complete sense of safety and security are optimally experienced. They include: being present, showing good intent and investing your strengths. Different levels of application or depth within each of these elements are demonstrated throughout all relationships, custodian to executive, leader to team members, team member to team member, team member to client and client to organizational organizations relations. Though generally understood, the amount of focus and action made towards them and the practice and execution of these elements is often downplayed in the face of clashing priorities or the drive towards immediate results. Each of these elements is examined in the next three sections.

Authenticity and Vulnerability

I did a study of 1500 executives at 200 organizations and, on average, only 55 percent of the employees know the organizations' main goals, 45 percent say it is clear what they are actually doing with their job, and only 43 percent say they can deal with the organization effectively if they need help. High-performing organizations have a 75-percent level of consistently shared goals. 72-percent rate for being clear what every employee's job is. 72 percent can ask for help, get what they need in a reasonable time to be successful. There's a tons and tons of data that if you work in a place where you really believe the majority adults controlling the place don't give a damn enough to tell you what's really going on, and correct any injustices, then the quality of your life at work is crap, your personal well-being is at danger. So, freaking, not telling you what's really is going on, it's inhumane. That kind of secrecy at work kills significant numbers of people.

Authenticity is critical for healthy discourse, diversity, and creativity. It is essential for self-awareness and empathy, too necessary components for complex communication and difficult discussions. It is part of the human connection. You will do better if the boss is mad at you for something you did than if the boss is mad at you for not meeting an expectation that you didn't know existed and violating a rule that you didn't even know was a rule and that you didn't agree with. Many of us will do more to avoid punishment ('protect your butt') than we will to move toward reward ('cover your heart'). What kind of life skills and competencies do we learn best and earliest? Those that are immediate, personal, and/or highly emotionally charged. What is rewarded and respected in most 'intellectual' endeavors? Those that are abstract, rational, and devoid of emotions. The early rewards and respect keep us from developing the later skills.

CHAPTER 4

Communication Skills

Let me stress the vital point: You must truly listen to the person you are conversing with. You cannot fake listening. A vital part of active listening is the ability to use your body well. Concentrate on the other person. This means not looking at yourself in the mirror or checking for missed calls on your phone. Make sure your conversation partner knows that you are paying attention to them for that moment. Keep your body open while sitting or standing so that you do not create a barrier between you and the other person. Remember to maintain eye contact. It is critical to making a person feel important and valuable. Furthermore, be open in your body language. Negative gestures make a person feel negative. Open gestures let them know that you are interested and responsive to their feelings. Political science tells us that over 70% of the communication process is achieved through body language. That is how important nonverbal communication is!

We live in a society with a lot of talking, but not a lot of listening. At social gatherings, people rarely sit down and converse for long periods. Our fast-paced way of life has made relationships very impersonal. By improving our communication skills, we can build solid, Kapuna-type relationships. It may be useful to reflect on what constitutes good communication. It is much more than just talking. Good communication involves both listening and speaking. In today's society, we seldom find someone who is willing to listen to us. Most of our friends are too busy interrupting us with their own ideas or comments.

Active Listening

Active listening is not just about hearing the weight. It also consists of non-verbal hints that we give to our friends that we actually care and are willing to participate in the conversation. Situations change, and eventually, this individual may be the one supporting us, and how would we want to speak if they felt half-hearted? Do we know that the concept of active listening and the power of listening are a skill that we can express off? Select the friends or family members who may benefit most from this active listening action if we find it hard to help. This allows us to learn the fundamentals of good listening and help us reach out more to others. The more we attempt to improve in every social situation, the better we should become. In addition, active listening requires our full concentration, and all of our energy is applied to the individual who tells the story.

The first step to problem solving is also to listen. We must listen to understand, not to respond. Sit there while the other person is speaking and do not talk. It is hard to make a judgment when we have not heard the whole story. Listening is the key to understanding. Often we allow our minds or emotions to predict what we do not have to say. We have no idea what the other person is thinking, and until we let them express the way they feel, we cannot always give them the support they need. People communicate so much by facing, sighing, and active engagement through facial expressions. These small, subtle actions are what can help a person overcome a difficult time and show them that we really care.

CHAPTER 5

Emotional Intelligence

In the Middle Ages, Leonardo DaVinci defined it as scientifically understanding what makes people happy. By the 19th and 20th centuries, toolmakers William McKinley and William James recognized the critical difference between people skills and technical skills, noting how important the former were to success in life. Using knowledge as a cultivation tool for their inner seeds of greatness, these individuals were not just leaders, they were guides, showing the way to a better life for their followers, instigating bursts of growth and hope. Over time, we have come to understand the importance of EQ (emotional intelligence) versus IQ for a happy and successful life.

I'm passionate about the topic of emotional intelligence as it bears heavily on the tenets and principles expressed in this book on what it means to be truly connected. It is this intelligence that allows us to understand and manage our own emotions, and to relate to the emotions of others. Emotionally intelligent people have the capacity to create positive, motivational contexts for themselves and others. Utilizing both the ability to understand and communicate with people, as well as the ability to direct oneself internally in communicating with all parties involved, they are able to help people feel appreciated and understood for the benefit of everyone. Daniel Goleman, a recognized expert and best-selling author on the subject of emotional intelligence, delves deeply into the subject of social competency, personal competency, and the neurological underpinning of social skills that universally rank as the top qualities sought after in leaders and designed to ensure performance with people at any age.

Self-Awareness and Empathy

Awareness of others It is generally agreed, in social science disciplines, that of all the formation processes of a leader's character, the development of empathy ought to be the top priority. Leadership attainment does not in itself develop empathy, nor does the realization of one's own significant role in the community; nor can a leader be brought closer to those of his society whose lives are most different from the norm without having personal knowledge of the suffering involved. Empathy, however, is profoundly muddied by a factor related to it: distress from others' states. Distress, unlike empathy, is the target of an assortment of situational variables and personality characteristics such as conceit (or its verbal form, arrogance), authoritarian control, and jealousy.

Awareness of self Self-awareness is the point of departure for outstanding leadership. Without this capacity, there's little reason to build skill in the other four areas with which we are concerned, for effective leadership presupposes that we know ourselves, our own needs, our own rights, and our own outlet for expression. There is an old management truism that says, "Don't try to sell a product you don't believe. Don't offer something you don't own." It's the same with leadership. Effective leaders are not secretly driven by lower order needs of which they are unaware, nor do their real needs conflict with the demands of the situation. They possess insight, not blindness; they can deal with reality. Finally, and most broadly, they are not on a search for identity.

CHAPTER 6

Cultivating Trust

Cultivate trust by: - Doing what you promise - Being consistent - Being honest and transparent even when it hurts - Being loyal and protective of others - Try to understand the perspectives of others - Communicate effectively. It is up to you to ensure that the message is understood; it is not the responsibility of your audience to understand what you are saying. The way information about organizational matters is communicated has a significant impact on morale and staff attitudes. Negative news can help if handled openly and truthfully; increases anxiety if glossed over; damages trust if hidden. Rumors always fill communication vacuums and are harder to dispel than put in place. Ensure that everyone is kept up-to-date with information about their work and workplace, especially if it might affect their well-being. Address staff concerns promptly. People quickly lose confidence in your ability if it appears there has been no reaction to issues that matter to the workforce.

Trust is the underpinning of all relationships. Appointments, titles, and positions are not enough. People want to have confidence in your reliability, integrity, and ability. Trust is a two-way street. You need it as much as others. Apart from the associated peace of mind, trust has a ripple effect on organizational performance. People in high-trust organizations are more open and collaborative, are better team players, perform better, and generally enjoy their work more. Where there is a trust vacuum, the aftermath is isolation, disengagement, and passive-aggressive behavior.

Consistency and Reliability

To qualify as a go-to person, you must be consistent in your judgment, be able to withstand the haste with humility, and present a reliable, targeted set of publications or ideas to improve, edify, and stimulate growth. If you have garnered the reputation as the person capable of presenting a reliable and accurate evaluation and judgment, you will notice that the way in which people relate and communicate with you will change. They will become more genuine, open, and willing to reciprocate. People are less intimidated by those who are quick to say "thank you" and respect accorded to true relationship leaders. You will witness a steady and sustained quickening in the people around you. These people recognize consistency in others because it is an ever-increasing trait in themselves.

Consistency and reliability are the characteristics less often emphasized when we think about building networks, but these are traits that will build your character and stand you in very good stead in all your relationships. You may delight the people in your sphere by introducing them to new and interesting ideas or social circles. This is stimulating and enjoyable. But being the go-to person who is gifted in helping and guiding and accepting consistent, reliable advice is what really counts. Your ability to predict personal and societal transitions and help other people navigate through is critical for their successful thriving. You have to be consistent in order to earn that honored position. You can't just read one article or take out this year and not follow up with an analysis.

CHAPTER 7

Resolving Conflict

Although voicing your feelings of frustration or anger, and feeling secure that your partner can do the same, are important, unresolved hostility is a relationship poison. It's important to find some tools to channel hostility in a constructive way. I have found that the power of humor sometimes can be used to dissipate any anger. One suggestion is for partners to first touch the other affectionately in order to express love or caring. Then they should focus on the positive aspects within themselves or within the other person, understanding that though one may feel angry at the moment, love and care are the motivators behind the argument. With this in mind, a person can express feelings of anger without fear or destructive retaliation, because they "fit" within the confines of love and caring.

To resolve conflicts as a couple, each person needs to be able to see things from the partner's perspective and show a willingness to compromise. I believe that the ability to work through a conflict and arrive at a mutually satisfactory resolution is the first big test of any relationship. When I am told by clients, "We never fight," I often think, "But how do you know your love is real?" I know they haven't experienced the intensity of feeling that accompanies a passionate conflict. I become concerned when there seems to be a lack of sufficient emotion present to support conflict and when small repeated disagreements are unresolved. Such deadness is a sign that the partnership hasn't yet strengthened by negotiation and compromise.

Effective Conflict Resolution Strategies

Being aware of personal attitude, conflict management strategies, and active listening is not enough to build and maintain successful relationships with others. The key to making these resources useful lies in the process of self-discovery, the individual development that takes a vague awareness of these resources and turns that awareness into specific skills that can be used in different situations to influence others in ways that strengthen existing relationships or form new connections.

Prepare by thinking about how you want to approach the person and the issue. Be aware of the importance of maintaining the relationship. 2. Begin with a neutral comment or question. Avoid labels or accusations, blaming, attacking, or threatening. Watch for negative nonverbal signals. Keep your language simple, direct, and neutral. Stick to the point. Be respectful. 3. Listen carefully to understand the other person's position. Paraphrase the other person's ideas occasionally, but listen more than you talk. Show understanding through nonverbal signals. 4. Empathize with the other person's feelings if possible. Develop trust in the relationship. Use respectful nonverbal signals. Be aware of nonverbal signals you are sending that may be negative and adjust them to match your thoughts. 5. Develop a possible solution or work together to reach a mutually satisfactory solution. The journey to this destination may appear like steps back and forth, but persistence is important. Suggest alternative solutions if possible. Openly discuss each alternative solution. Request or state commitment from the other person. Demonstrate understanding and empathy. 6. Approach with care when you revisit the conflict.

Struggling with the same steps in the same way finally may bring success. Demonstrate understanding and empathy. Be respectful.

The prospect of conflict can close the door to too many potential relationships that do not need to be lost. Therefore, it is essential to develop strategies that promote the successful resolution of conflict. Some steps to consider when conflict is a possibility are as follows:

CHAPTER 8

Nurturing Relationships Over Time

In all our interactions with people, no matter how small, connections are an opportunity to deepen the relationship. So, making a conscious effort to do so in the normal course of the day and when we can find opportunities socially ensures that relationships we care about continue to expand and grow. To nurture a solid web of connectedness around us and to maintain meaningful relationships, it is important to keep in touch regularly, a little bit each time, so that people can trust and rely on us, as we feel they can. To maintain and nurture relationships, it is essential to make it a habit, an unthinking way of life, and the impact is both subtle and deep, supporting our own well-being and the well-being of society around us.

Nurturing relationships over time is not something we tend to think about, but it is not just about maintaining relationships in the sense of keeping in touch. All relationships evolve, and whether they grow in positive ways or wither depends on what we do. Nurturing connections is essential to maintaining close relationships, and it requires conscious effort. People we see often or associate with regularly are normally the ones we have good relationships with. By being intentional about it, we can enhance this.

Investing in Quality Time

Despite these formidable challenges, the pursuit of a different agenda that attempts to balance out material gains with more meaningful adult and child connections will ultimately result in a higher degree of family and social stability and a more optimistic future. The key to achieving a larger quotient of meaningful family time is to capitalize on the "big blocks of connectivity" that already exist within the family structure. These blocks consist of the work, interaction, and relaxation patterns that match the operating units of families and result in a minimum of lost or stressed time during the workweek. Time spent together should be looked upon as the source of enjoyment and pleasure, and not simply as a chore to be processed. The end objective should be to develop routine, ordinary, and common connections, using any available fragments of time that become available.

The most significant investment that a person can make in their relationships is the investment of quality time. Impersonal and detached connections result from the consumption of large quantities of small units of time through services, entertainment, and speedy or serial conversations. The sharing of a few units of large and meaningful blocks of time will create the exchange of caring, affirmation, understanding, and confidence and produce momentous connections of depth and intimacy. Unfortunately, the demands of work, the tasks of life, and the challenges of survival drain time away from people, and the process of reducing existing time units down to smaller portions diminishes it even more.

CHAPTER 9

The Role of Technology

At various times over the past several centuries, we've witnessed skepticism of and even disdain for labor-saving and leisure-enhancing technology, warnings about the potential uses of technology by exploiters, and a longing for "earlier and less frantic" times. At various times over the past several centuries, we've heard leaders talking of alienation from the people and soul-destroying effects of excessive reliance on communications technology. And various generations have wondered about the potential negative effects of an unprecedented ability to communicate, particularly on social life, democratic processes, family gatherings, and the more personal side of life. And there are some who have feared a net dislocation of the work force and social upheaval through the technological elimination of skilled jobs. Are we shaking our heads yet?

Let's end where we all know we will: the subject of technology. While we have referred to the role of technology and social media throughout this book, now is the time to address the many questions and concerns we often hear from business leaders about technology and connection. We will begin with an incredibly profound and important statement you have absolutely no reason to believe, at least initially. That is, every particular question or concern that you or anyone else can possibly conjure up about technology, social media, and the current obsession with the virtual side of life has been pondered and articulated before about a previous dominant technology: the printing press, the telephone, the telegraph, radio, television, the personal computer, the telecommunication revolution. When the potential leadership restraints of telecommuting or telecommuting will come to pass, that didn't. The Internet.

Balancing Virtual and In-Person Interactions

A cautionary tale: I was once very involved with a bloggers' community, using the same name as I am here. The virtual community that built up around the site and its new owner was amazing. We met twice a year in person as well. There were conversations late into the night at these meet-ups, lots of funny stories, good wine and good food, and we caught up with what was going on in one another's lives in person. But the power of the group was much, much less when we were not able to do those in-person events. In the intervening years, I have very tenuous connections to these people and became close to only one of them in real life. It's not that all of my virtual friends aren't wonderful people, but gardens aren't built on people that we only email with or leave comments for online. They're built with people that we work hard with, whose faces and voices we recognize, and with whom we can share our dips into negativity and leaps into happiness. They require being open and authentic. If we focus only on our online connections and don't make choosing the location unconditional enough, we miss out on taking advantage of the unique rewards that in-person relationships offer.

The last consideration in this chapter is finding a balance between virtual and in-person interactions. Admittedly, easier for some of us than others (I struggle with being responsive to long-distance relationships, but I'm not alone), we should be aware that no group of virtual friends will ever replace our in-person connections.

CHAPTER 10

Building Professional Relationships

When many well-meaning people surround you in your leadership role, you can end up being overcommitted, exhausted, vulnerable, and maybe even verbally harassed during the times you would have sought comfort or solace. The importance here is to also develop relationships with those who do not know or understand your role within the institution. That is not to say that you are not to have established relationships with your leadership team, or to sustain relationships with the institution's faculty, staff, or student constituents.

Self-disclosure is an important part of the human-to-human relationship-building process. However, there is a time and place for all things. Disclose in stages to prevent burnout, overcommitments, or the potential to be. Keep some part of yourself private as a buffer against those times when you may be under attack, and you will need some private thoughts to comfort and protect you.

Be patient with people who struggle with accepting your leadership. Much of the time, their frustration lies not with you, but with the expectations and demands they process as a part of their respective roles within the Academy.

Remember that everyone has something valuable to offer, and that may include unfollowing the crowd. Independent thinkers can, and often will, make important and significant contributions. Here are a few additional tips and insights to consider when building relationships.

Networking Strategies

Be ready. Be ready to quickly, yet adequately and thoughtfully, explain what you do, and what your mission is. Present yourself in a friendly, clear, and enthusiasm-building manner. Be understandable. Make your statements and messages clear and thoughtfully presented. Confirm your understanding of what is being communicated to you. Demonstrate understanding of your message. Demonstrate an interest in learning more. Clarifying and paraphrasing that you understand their message adds value to your interaction. Yes, the ability to acknowledge and build upon by affirming information. Chances are, it was worth it! Be conversant. Follow-up on the discussions you have. You don't need to know everything about most things; just know where to find the expertise. Include key constituency groups. Know your contacts and their interest in issues, people, and communities. Keep the bigger picture unsurpassed. Grow and enhance your network. Keep looking for a potential team.

Welcoming. Be more welcoming with the people you meet. This will make it easier for you to start relationships. When we feel welcomed, we are more positive, engaged, committed to participating, and willing to consider new ideas, and we learn better. Be sure to listen attentively, truly listen, when others are speaking. When we truly listen, we pay full attention to others, understand their feelings and defer judgment. A warm and inviting networker is personally accessible and takes a curious interest in others. A warm and inviting networker actively listens and encourages others to talk. A warm and inviting networker is open, supportive, and approachable. Be genuinely interested. When you are interested and genuinely give your time to others, they are more likely to share the essence of their thoughts and feelings with you. This is a powerful and unique part of human interaction.

CHAPTER 11

Relationships in Different Contexts

The key to the formative power that interactions can have on the development of ideas lies in whether the process of interaction allows for elaboration or changes in the mental model that the person at the other side holds. Research on peer learning identifies the active exchange of reasoning and the resolution of disagreement or disjoint interpretations as key processes for the kind of interaction that prompts learning. It is clear, from this work and from our case study examples, that the development of relational creativity in face-to-face and computer-mediated learning will rely on active interaction between people whose ideas are valued by each other, and that relationships must be continually reconstructed through the ongoing exchange and assessment of each other's interpretation over time.

Relationships are built in diverse contexts. We have emphasized a number of domains specific to education and learning. However, some concepts that we have covered can be generalized. This chapter describes some of the implications that our analysis holds for dynamics in other domains. We start with one example of meaningful interaction and close with a brief discussion of relationships in romantic settings.

Family Relationships

Most people have family members with whom they have difficulty, although the person may be a beloved family friend, relative, or spouse. Because the relationship is especially important to us emotionally and because of its long history, wounds, and misjudgments, these relationships can seem especially difficult to manage. They do not have to entail stinging barbed disputes, distance, unresolved feelings or needs, or malicious efforts to inflict suffering. They can be and should ultimately be one of the most important sources of pleasure in our life. Therefore, we should treat the family with the utmost respect, love, and understanding, especially when difficult times or difficulties with temporary or long-term repair exist. Keep in mind that the priority and completeness of the relationship should ensure the collaboration of both sides.

Family is the place where we first learned about relationships, trust, love, emotional bonding, and caring. It is a place that has the greatest impact on the essence of who we are and who we are able to become. But unless these initial relationships are good, they lead to a whole system of distorted experiences and emotional pain. We often learn a very narrow concept of love. Our concept of ourselves and our worth depends greatly on our early relationships within our family. As a result, we take a giant step toward happiness when we are able to change the dynamics within our original family by loving ourselves and others, by allowing our wounds and others' wounds to heal, and by integrating our creative, spontaneous real self into a significant member of the family.

CHAPTER 12

Cultural Considerations

The focus on the power of relationships has led to broad acceptance of the idea that both intrinsic and extrinsic goals are required for comprehensive well-being. Well-being is less about what people have in possession, such as clothing or technological items, as it is about the relationships that people have. Preoccupation with material items distracts people from building strong connections. This should be seen as both a work and a life issue. It is a personal problem for people who hoard possessions, and it means that people substitute material items for relationships, resulting in more worker alienation and less friendliness at work.

Because a variety of cultural traditions emphasize the importance of developing deep connections with others, it is likely that many or most cultures in the world emphasize the development of social relatedness as a key characteristic for individuals. Thus, around the world, people seem to understand their personal development in part through their interaction with others. The specific definition and the particular rules and customs surrounding the process of relatedness are culturally determined, however. This has important implications for people who are responsible for helping others to develop meaning in their lives, especially when working with people from cultural backgrounds different from their own.

Understanding Cross-Cultural Communication

What happens in cross-cultural communication, then, is that we are seeing and interpreting the world based on our own cultural norms with little awareness of or accommodation made for the behaviors, values, and norms of the people we're dealing with. Since communication is a two-way street, people from different cultures bring their own ideas of the "right" way to talk, act, and respond in a business situation. If you don't understand and accommodate the communication motivations of the people you are dealing with, you'll have difficulty building the relationships necessary to conduct business. In business, cross-cultural communication is necessary to prevent misunderstandings that have the potential to seriously damage business relationships and business success. In this module, we explore some of the many areas of miscommunication that can cause problems in business relationships. We also offer a variety of guidelines and techniques for minimizing or avoiding the potential misunderstandings.

As businesses become increasingly global, people from different cultures are interacting more than ever. The increase in both foreign business and study means that many of our regions are becoming increasingly multicultural. Each of us is shaped by our past experiences, our values, and our ways of perceiving and thinking that are ingrained in us. These internal factors exert considerable power in determining our communication patterns and responses, not only in how we act and react but also in understanding the other person. The more we understand these aspects of ourselves, the more successful we are in establishing rapport and mutual understanding with people from other cultures.

CHAPTER 13

The Impact of Social Media

Substantive studies have yet to be fully accomplished to address the superficial and imitative qualities of interaction it has taken the place of. The few studies that have been undertaken are of concern to us all. The risks relating to social media are based on changes in the essence of social interaction rather than the possibilities of harm created by actual interaction. At the very best, social media might serve as a supplement in social relationships; at its worst, men, women, and children might be more harmed by people with whom they have superficial or no real relationships. The danger is this. As Hillel has maintained, the Torah teaches us to be a kind, caring, and thoughtful people. We can only manifest those attributes in how we treat people we know and how we treat people who have done nothing to merit our kindness. Will we lose that kindness, thoughtfulness, caring, and respect for others if more social interactions do not happen face-to-face?

Maintaining Authenticity Online

There is beauty in our two-way disconnect. We understand the differences between our real and digital selves and choose how to intertwine them. Digitally, we use technology to enhance our individualism and express ourselves on a fuller, more independent level. We still preserve the space to consider our relationships, rather than acting on them. Time away from physical interaction allows us to gain this introspection and even evaluate the relationships where face-to-face connectivity is strongest. As with most human interaction and its complexity, there are natural limits to the process. We may start adjusting those limits and begin to strip the infrastructure off when we dampen the intensity and depth of our emotional online lives. Regardless, we will still value opportunities to switch off and manage our ever-increasing digital relationships, while searching for ways to transcend these inherent boundaries between our in-person and online selves.

In both professional settings and personal interactions, there is often a stigma attached to openly professing emotions over digital mediums. While we have learned how to use emoticons and capital letters to add affect into our texts, the ultimate experience still lacks physical cues and overt excitability. As a result, we often hold our emotions back. Most may think this is a disadvantage of communicating over digital mediums. I choose to think it is a reminder of our intrinsic selves. Despite the sway of external influences, we still value fundamental emotions and the human experience. This debate reveals our dual nature as humans: how much technology we have integrated already, and how small the boundaries between our online interactions are maintained. It comes down to a question of continuous identity and whether we can maintain authenticity when online relationships have been digitized.

CHAPTER 14

Mentorship and Guidance

Throughout our conversation, I weaved components of the Nargis Model into a more generic, strategic approach to mentorship and guidance. The Nargis Model has an emphasis on presenting to the community; it provides opportunities for scholars to voice their professional goals to a network of individuals outside Generation. In addition, scholars forge personal relationships with the public versus private sectors and all programs support public speaking, which can act as a powerful leadership tool. These components work in concert with a message that underscores the importance of relationship building and not just referring to only one individual as a mentor.

During interviews, I often get asked about my mentors and individuals that have guided me throughout my career journey. Many of the young leaders who ask me this question have little or no guidance on how to identify or establish a mentor. When I was climbing the corporate ladder, I also exhibited a lot of the same misguided tendencies. I wanted to have the right mentor for the right reason and I wanted to have the picture-perfect relationship. That script looks like: Take note that this is in order and it is important to uphold this order, older, professional, same career, and older again. If that were not enough, a recent college graduate asked me for a more realistic approach to mentorship because she was having a hard time finding any mentor at all. A major perk of being in the Nargis Twelfth Grade Academy (TGA) Program is mentorship so, as I spoke with her, I realized that there are many individuals out there who may grapple with these same challenges.

The Benefits of Mentorship

A mentor can be someone in your same profession, someone in a similar career, or even someone with a similar background. It can be someone in your family, someone who has overcome similar circumstances, or someone who merely has the wisdom you need. Your mentor is your crucial connection, the person who can answer every question you have. With a little guidance and love, you can have a truly extraordinary life. The nature of a mentor is to share, and there are so many talented, educated people out there who would love to help you step onto the best path toward your brightest future. Vastly improving your understanding of the world around you, a mentor can help you choose the best career for you by providing you with the benefit of her experience, guiding you down your chosen avenue of study, and, ultimately, helping you build the life of your dreams.

If you want to make your life more successful, inspiring, and fulfilling, then you need to be aware of one of the most magical concepts of our time: mentorship. If you do not already have a mentor in your life, one of the first steps you can take to create a better life is to find one. It only has to be one person, and this one person can change your life. In fact, in many cases - if you have the right mentor and the right relationship - finding one such person to mentor you can be all you really need to have what can nearly amount to a complete education. A mentor is someone older than you who has been in your shoes. Someone who has been through the goals you are setting. Someone who has been through the challenges you are facing. Someone who is willing to share everything he or she has learned with you.

CHAPTER 15

Self-Reflection and Growth

As you pursue your own development, remember to dialogue with the other person as well. Discuss the insights you are gaining about yourself, and become interested in the other's growth. This will frequently lead to the discovery of common ground between the two of you. The simple practice of comparing your developmental path with that of someone else can illuminate personal growth opportunities for both of you. Such information exchange represents a special kind of dialogue: in a sense, a more intense form of cooperative feedback. This approach actually helps people to come to know who they are and who they may grow to become, with greater freedom and insight into their own learning process.

Each of these methods provides a different avenue that leads toward personal growth, but they have as their common goal a greater realization of our strengths and challenges so that we can expand our further development of the gifts we bring to our relationships.

- Set the intention to develop, learn, open up. - Treat yourself like a good friend. - Express yourself more authentically. - Listen more deeply and skillfully. - Get feedback. - Take the Enneagram. - Use 360-degree feedback. - Identify your core shadow qualities. - The Johari window. - Create an environment that fosters personal development. - Recovery through change and the coaching relationship.

Personal growth is the key to maintaining the health and vitality of our relationships. When we are growing and expanding in various dimensions, our relationships will be enriched. Our growth will take different forms at different times. At times we will focus intently on growth related to specific issues and needs that are not being met. Sometimes we will be spontaneously growing, often in a related domain or a more global way.

Learning from Past Relationships

When assessing past relationships, some people find it helpful to do a self-assigned "what went wrong" and "what went right" exercise. One writes down everything that went right, either in one relationship or in relationships overall. Then a person writes down everything that went wrong. These lists provide us with an opportunity to learn about our wants, needs, and the things that scare us in relationships. It is my belief that primary relationships have much to teach us. They are a mirror to our very soul.

Even past relationships that were difficult can provide us with wisdom, not only about our partner but also about ourselves. We can ask ourselves: What has been my experience in past relationships? What kinds of relationships do I seek out? Why? What patterns come up in my relationships? How do I communicate, deal with differences, and seek closeness? It is important to understand this in order to be accountable to ourselves, to increase our self-awareness, and to be present and authentic. One way to do this is to focus on feelings that come up in relationships, such as doubts, fears, and feelings of vulnerability. Then we can ask what meaning those feelings have for us.

CHAPTER 16

The Power of Gratitude

Use present affirmations in your relationship. Say out loud gratitude statements, and you will maintain a healthy and loving relationship. This will make expressing your gratitude and appreciation towards your partner and loved ones habitual for both of you. All good relationships are really built on the foundation of acceptance and gratitude, as they nourish all the beautiful qualities associated with love, such as the sweet, warm, kind, and highly cherished actions leading to greater happiness, peace, and positivity overall.

To reap the true benefits, no rules or formulae are needed except a true intention to accept things the way they are; worrying won't get you anywhere. Many people throughout the ages have said that constantly speaking gratitude guarantees 100% success in their relationships, but this is not the case for some other people. Just the occasional appreciation and gratitude shows them that you still care. A good way to begin the expression of gratitude and appreciation is by looking around at the small, ordinary things in life that we normally take for granted. These things actually make our lives more meaningful and satisfying.

Expressing Appreciation

What had occurred to me would seem like second nature to some people. In my younger years, I'd said thanks perhaps more often. Maybe it was living in polite Canada, where everyone says they're sorry and thank you for every little thing, that desensitized me. Or perceptive university professors whose carefully disguised sarcasm trained me to be more politically correct. I have, over the years, noticed a correlation between a lack of genuineness and the "sorry"/"thank you" epidemic. The Drake-Poehler Sorry video had certainly struck a chord, with its numerous celebrities poking fun at Canadians. I jokingly attribute the film's wild success to snow-bound Canuck solidarity, where viewers could email an apology to their buddies no questions asked. But I do believe that there is a grain of truth in this. I'll let you, gentle reader, decide for yourselves. However, I'll continue my daily thank-you practice until the end of this book. What do you have to lose by joining me for just 30 days? When we start to live with a little more gratitude, the world becomes a richer and happier place. When we bond with words that praise, others notice and begin to do the same.

It sounded like something that came out of Dale Carnegie's "How to Win Friends and Influence People." Perhaps I'd been reading one too many self-help books. A blog I follow extolled the virtues of expressing appreciation. What did I have to lose? I could start juicing up the thank-yous right away. It didn't have to be any-thing grandiose, just a thank-you for something specific, each day, either in person or in writing. A daily appreciation tweet would also work. Although doing something daily is not usually my thing—I scarcely expected to still be blogging after 100 days—I decided to give it a shot. How well could I thank someone for something every day for the same period? I'd experienced huge paybacks from other self-discipline mechanisms such as my 365-day meditation chal-lenge. Besides, I knew that I was somewhat on the stingy side about expressing my thanks, usually because the trigger guys were getting for the wrong reasons.

CHAPTER 17

Conclusion

Cultural theory is important for sociology and the concepts of sense of being and consciousness are crucial for TEPS students and teachers because everyone is a social being and has questions about being. Sociologists and teachers who critically contemplate their dominant cultural orders and ways of thinking will be more attentive and proactive in creating meaningful relationships. Sociologists know that their communities and schools are the loci of social justice and equity and contribute to the formation of consensual identities by way of continuous and authentic conversations about human dignity, relationships, and moral codes.

Although sociology is the foundation of discussion and theory in this book, both of us are committed to creating conditions inside and outside the classroom that foster caring, mutual respect, and communicative action. As social beings, we thrive when living in communion with others by means of meaningful relationships, and our societies thrive when they recognize and respect the signs that we find deep and rich meaning in our connectedness with others. The cultural theory of the three social orders is just one way of understanding the manner in which people relate to others in the world because it is woven from the threads of language, cognition, law, and relationships. Language, for instance, provokes and defies our sense of being and consciousness because we use symbols to communicate and represent whether or not we are aware of potential consequences. The balance between sense of being and consciousness influences our sense of morality, justice, and equitable relationships with others and with the cosmos.

The Lifelong Journey of Building Meaningful Relationships

Many students (particularly the nonundergraduates) noted that they will have future opportunities to explore and work through future challenges and potentialities in relationships and reflecting on these questions and, once experienced, see beyond the role of a leader to understand interpersonal dynamics during the process. As I reflect on that text and following the readings in our first week of class, all of the potential energy we began developing and reflecting on began to blossom into something more powerful and less manipulative or competitive. Decolonizing gender theologians remind us about the transformative power and possibilities of relationships: A new world of worldwide solidarity is other possible, a world where environmental justice, economic justice, racial justice, gender justice, and various other forms of social justice are attainable.

Relationship building is a lifelong journey of growth through various experiences. Being socialized into gendered family structures shapes individuals and could shape the dynamics of their personal relationships. In "But how do you form this baby? How do you teach others," we touched on the concepts of creating relationships and working closely together through team building. As a PhD student, many boundaries were crossed, many others were strengthened, and I am currently learning to build even stronger relationships. In my reflections, I invited students to demonstrate a willingness and potential to challenge themselves and to start to develop a self-awareness and commitment to working in a group. Shifting the group's dynamic in the most successful such experiences appeared to create conditions whereby the potentiality for quick, deep, authentic energetic connection and relationships could be cultivated.

All semester long, we have been talking about building and nurturing meaningful relationships through our nature and nurture class. One of the first things we discussed as a class was the deep craving that people have for human connection. The concept of wanting to be connected with other people is not something many of us knew we had prior to taking this class. I still hear about it from my colleagues when they speak about their own experiences in the class. There is a huge part of me that wants to call bs on them because I realized I was at that craving stage and really wanted a friendship like the one the professor brought up. I knew this without the reading I did about the power of connection and relationships. It seems that many of the students in my program knew this concept prior to being introduced to it but 16 weeks later were questioning and discussing their gendered families about the processing of getting together and the act of processing together. I see it happen in all of our outside readings. We learn to be more honest, open, and revealed being with one another.